Beyond The Surface

A Poetry book by
Ebosetae Okoyo

Copyright © 2024 By Ebosetae Ann Okoyo. All rights reserved.

No part of this book may be reproduced, distributed, or transmitted in any form or by any means, including photocopying, recording, or other electronic or mechanical methods, without the prior written permission of the publisher, except in the case of brief quotations embodied in critical reviews and certain other noncommercial uses permitted by copyright law.

Dear Readers,

It is with great pleasure that I present to you this collection of poetry that is very dear to my heart. Each poem has been crafted with love, honesty, and vulnerability. They represent my journey through life, love, loss, healing and self-discovery. I hope they will resonate with you, inspire you, and perhaps even provide you with a sense of comfort.

As you read through these pages, you will find pieces that talk about the depth of heartbreak, healing, self-love, the tranquility of finding peace within and everything in between. You will find poems that are raw and unfiltered, and others that are uplifting and full of hope. But all of them have one thing in common: they come from a place of authenticity and truth.

When I first started writing these poems, I had no intention of sharing them with the world. They were simply a way for me to process my thoughts and emotions. But as I continued to write, I realized that these words had the power to touch others and make a difference in their lives. So, I decided to gather them all in one place and share them with you.

My hope is that these poems will not only offer you a glimpse into my personal journey but will also encourage you to explore your own emotions and experiences. That these poems will serve as a reminder that you are not alone in your struggles. That even in the darkest moments, there is still light to be found. That your pain is not your identity, and that healing is possible. That you are worthy of love, respect, and all the good things life has to offer.

Thank you for taking the time to read my words. I invite you to sit back, relax, and immerse yourself in the beauty of words. I hope that this collection of poems brings you joy, comfort, healing and inspiration.

With love,

Ebosetae x.

Table of Contents

CRACKS IN THE ARMOUR 1
- FOUL PLAY 3
- WHAT DOES HEARTBREAK FEEL LIKE? 4
- TEARY NIGHT 5
- ENOUGH 6
- MEMORIES 7
- UNCONSCIOUS 8
- DESPAIR 9
- INTERNAL WOES 10
- MONOLOGUE: REMINISCING 11
- UNANSWERED QUESTIONS 13
- LOVE IN A PARALLEL WORLD 14
- 1:04AM 15
- BE GONE, YOU NARCISSIST 16

IN THE EYE OF THE STORM 18
- REFLECTIONS OF SELF 20
- MONOLOUGE: UNFULFILLED 22
- COMPANION 24
- WAKE UP (A POEM FOR QUEENS) 25
- LONG ROAD 26
- I GOT FLOWERS TODAY 27
- I CAN SEE THE LIGHT 28
- MONOLOGUE: CAN I BE HONEST I 30
- LOVE & WAR 31
- DAYDREAMING 32
- REPEAT FEELINGS 33
- ECHOS OF REGRET 34
- LOST AND FOUND 35
- THE BEST REVENGE 36
- MONOLOGUE: LET IT OUT 37

MIDNIGHT MUSINGS 39
- SELFISH LOVE 41
- BEAUTIFUL MAN 42

FANTASY LOVE 43
HEY, STRANGER 44
IF I HAD A MAN 45
SINS OF THE NIGHT 46
MONOLOGUE: CAN I BE HONEST II 47
TIME WILL NOT WAIT FOR YOU 48
MY LOVER 49
WINGS OF ENVY 50
EMBRACING SILENCE 51
TO BE 52
BOUND BY DESIRE 53
ILLUSIONS OF LUST 54
TIMELESS DEVOTION 56

RISING FROM THE ASHES 58

SCARS AND STARDUST 60
THEY HEARD YOU 61
LET GO 62
NEW BEGINNINGS 63
ALL THE THINGS YOU ARE 64
THE ACT OF FREEDOM 65
I AM 66
CONSTANT REMINDER 67
RADIANT RESILIENCE 68
MONOLOGUE: ALMOST THERE 69
STANDING IN THE MIRROR 71
DEFINE 72
OCEAN BREEZE 74
SHEDDING 76
LET'S TALK 78
POTRAITS OF PEACE 80
STRENGTH THROUGH THE STORM 81
FREE AT LAST 82

LOVE LETTERS 83

DEAR YOUNGER ME, ... 84
"HOW WOULD YOU LIKE TO BE LOVED?" 86
TOO MUCH 87
SWEET LOVE 88

A PRAYER FOR YOU 89
LETTER TO MY UNBORN (a poem for V) 90
A MOTHER'S LOVE (a poem for my mum) 91
WHAT WOULD IT FEEL LIKE TO FIND GENUINE
LOVE? 93
LETTER TO MY READERS, PART I 94
LETTER TO MY READERS, PART II 95
REMEMBER 96

CRACKS IN THE ARMOUR

FOUL PLAY

He was everything and more,
Or so she thought,
Filled with sweet nothings,
And beautiful lies,
Hidden agendas behind his smiles,
His voice so soothing –
The roots of his deception

She knew all this,
Yet chose to stay,
Maybe it was the way he looked at her,
With those deceitful eyes,
Or the way he held her,
With arms that had been felt by everyone else,
Or maybe he had charmed her,
With the venom that he spat every time his mouth opened.

Whatever it was,
It was like a drug,
That she one day hoped to sober up from

WHAT DOES HEARTBREAK FEEL LIKE?

First there's numbness.

A disbelief that stretches every second,

The world feels distant, sounds muffled,

And the heart, it just doesn't understand.

Then anger, raw and unfiltered.

Questions without answers,

A clenched fist, a tight chest,

A yearning to rewind the hands of time

A battle within yourself, quiet whispers.

Maybe if I had said this, done that,

A hope that we can somehow negotiate with the past.

Then a heavy weight settles in, depression.

Days start to fade, time slows down,

The world, once vibrant, now gray,

And the silence, it's deafening.

But slowly, acceptance begins to set in.

Understanding that endings are also beginnings,

That love, though changed, remains,

And the heart learns to breathe again.

TEARY NIGHT

3 a.m. on a rainy and windy night

I didn't expect to cry tonight

But my tears have become an overflowing river

Sweeping through your city

Taking down everything in its path

Destroying walls made with pieces of a broken heart,

Buildings tainted with insincere apologies,

Roads paved with painful memories,

Trees growing with malicious intent.

With each teardrop, the water rises.

And until the city is submerged,

The tears won't stop.

ENOUGH

What does it mean to be enough?

Her mind's eye races through time

Flipping through the pages of past resolutions

Life has a droll way of ridiculing us

Pain morphs into fear

And that which you feared becomes that which you fear,

Consequently making us our own nemesis

Degrading our moral compass

Constantly asking if we're good enough

Rendering us worthless, hopeless

Begging to be freed.

Yet in reality, we are our own prisoners

Shackled to our minds inability to define what it means to be enough.

MEMORIES

In a moment of terror and confusion,

She found herself pinned against the wall,

Her attacker's hands tight around her neck,

Eyes devoid of humanity,

Mouth filled with accusations and venom.

In a desperate attempt to fight back,

She lunged forward, but collided with the table,

Feeling the impact echo through her body.

As the chaos subsided, he tried to brush it off,

Blaming her for what had happened,

Leaving her questioning her sanity.

Eventually, she apologized for his actions,

But deep down she knew it was not her fault.

UNCONSCIOUS

Conscious yet unconscious,

Eyes open slowly to a stark reality,

A room sealed tight, filled with emptiness and mirrors,

The deafening silence intensified the demons within,

Every imperfection and flaw laid out bare before her,

Heart racing, breaths shallow.

A stronghold tightening its grip,

As the air became scarce, her struggle intensified,

Until she broke free,

Only to find herself trapped in another room,

The cycle repeating itself over and over again.

Conscious yet unconscious,

Trapped in a cycle of unhappiness,

But perhaps the key to escape lies within.

DESPAIR

From the depths of despair,
When her world fell apart,
She was alone and heavy in heart
Her life had been shattered by
A tight-fisted hand
Who could she turn to?
Who would understand?

With no self-esteem and in a broken mess
She made a decision about her happiness
She gathered all the courage she could find
To make a stand for herself and leave him behind

Those first few months were the loneliest she'd ever been
But she knew it was worth it not to be hurt again
In finding herself, she cried a river of tears
Learning to love herself and facing her fears.

INTERNAL WOES

Battered by the scuffles of life

Choked in desolation

Scars that reveal past woes

Partly healed lacerations reopened

by flashbacks,

An ongoing battle internally

A perfectly put together exterior

-

If only they knew the half of it

If only they knew that this mask hid the misery so well

That she began to bask in the glory of it

It hid the torture so well

That she began to lead a double life

that held a conspiracy of silence

-

If only they knew.

MONOLOGUE: REMINISCING

Three years and a few months later, she loved him with every fiber of her being. Their love was the kind that made her believe in soulmates, and she felt deep down in her heart that he was the one. She had envisioned a future with him, their children, and a house with a white picket fence. Meeting each other's families seemed to confirm what she was feeling – he was the one for her. He had helped her forget her past, and she loved him more than anything else in this world.

She would have done anything for him. And he loved her just as deeply, showering her with affection and attention. They were compatible in every way, and she was convinced that this was God's plan for her life. She moved a million miles away just to be closer to him, thinking it was the right thing to do.

But everything changed when she discovered his infidelity and the terrible temper, he had kept hidden. She would always forgive him because, of course, she loved him. But she realized forgiveness was not the answer. It was unfathomable to her that someone she loved so much could hurt her so deeply, even though she had shown him nothing but love. Their relationship felt like it stood the test of time, but it also felt like a lifetime of love and pain.

He would never understand the depth of her hurt, as men sometimes think that women overreact to such things. Although he apologized countless times, he couldn't comprehend why she wouldn't take him back. Because even as deeply as she loved him, she couldn't keep losing parts of herself for him to find his.

He was the man she had imagined spending the rest of her life with, planning weddings and a life together. Because after their relationship ended, she found herself trying to find solace in temporary situations, hoping they would heal her broken heart. They never seemed to though. They just seemed to draw her further away from herself.

I know that many people can relate to the pain of betrayal and heartbreak. It's a feeling that cuts deep and leaves scars that never fully heal. But through it all, you learn that you are stronger than you ever imagined. You are strong for being able to pull yourself out even when your heart wants you to stay. You learn to trust your instincts and not ignore the red flags. And while you may never fully get over the pain sometimes, you know that you will survive, and someday, you will find a love that is worthy of you and the love you have to give.

UNANSWERED QUESTIONS

Will I ever feel love again,

the type that's unconditional?

The kind that brings fluttering butterflies?

Can I ever trust again?

That a "yes" means yes, and "no" means, no?

It's not that you're irreplaceable,

But my idea of love is tainted.

Replacing you seems impossible, not because you're the one,

But because my heart is desensitized, numb.

Is love forever lost to me, a thing of the past,

Or can it still find me, and make my heart beat fast?

LOVE IN A PARALLEL WORLD

Love can be unkind,

Crippling, and belittling,

Filling one's heart with fear.

It can be all that is not good,

A battlefield, brittle and shallow.

Love can bring anxiety,

Weakness, and endless worry,

An uncertainty of the future.

And when it fades,

It leaves one feeling empty.

But perhaps, in the end,

Love was never enough,

For it was never truly love.

Real love brings joy, peace,

And a sense of security,

A true treasure worth holding on to.

1:04AM

Is it possible to exhaust all tears?

Can a broken heart shatter even more?

Can life move on without me?

Is it intuition or just overthinking?

The battle within has brought great confusion.

Just when I thought my walls were impenetrable,

Did you easily thaw them down?

Just when I thought my heart had grown resilient,

Just when I thought I was safe,

So many pieces of my heart scattered on the cold floor.

I don't want to gather them this time.

I don't want to build any walls this time.

No more feelings, no more emotions,

Just an empty, heartless soul wandering.

BE GONE, YOU NARCISSIST

The world is but a stage

And the narcissist, the lead actor

Their ego, a fiery fire

That consumes all in its path

They'll charm and seduce with their words and cunning ways,

But don't be fooled by their facade,

A mask that soon deteriorates.

They crave attention and admiration,

A constant supply of their drug.

And if you dare to challenge them,

Oh! Be prepared for their constant antagonism.

They'll twist and turn reality to fit their own twisted view,

And leave you questioning your sanity,

Wondering if what they say about you is true.

Beware of the narcissist's enticing and manipulative ways.

Because in the end, it's all about them,

And the destruction they always cause.

IN THE EYE OF THE STORM

REFLECTIONS OF SELF

Sometimes I see myself in shades of grey,

Ridden with flaws and doubts,

A fractured mirror, pieces of shattered glass,

Reflecting a broken past.

But others see a different view,

They see a beautifully painted portrait

A canvas rich with hues and light

A masterpiece with no flaws

They see a strength that I fail to see

They see the beauty in my imperfections

-

So why can't I see that?

Why can't I see the worth & beauty deep in me?

Maybe it's fear that clouds my sight

A lingering lack of confidence maybe

-

I hope they can permit me to use their eyes

To witness these things they see in me

The strength beyond the pain

The beauty beyond the scars

Maybe then I'll finally be able to really see myself

Rather than the made-up idea created by my thoughts

MONOLOUGE: UNFULFILLED

I feel like I'm just not enough. Like I'm always falling short, never quite measuring up. No matter how hard I try, no matter how much I achieve, there's always this nagging sense that it's not enough.

And it's not just about external achievements - it's about who I am as a person. Am I kind enough? Am I thoughtful enough? Am I generous enough? The answer, always, seems to be no.

I look around me and see other people doing amazing things, achieving great success, making a real difference in the world. And I wonder - why can't I be like that? Why can't I do something truly great, something that will make a real impact?

And then there's the sense of unfulfillment. Like there's something missing, something I can't quite put my finger on. I go through the motions of life - work, relationships, hobbies - but it all feels a bit hollow. Like I'm just going through the motions, but not really living.

I know I should be grateful for what I have. I have a good job, a loving family, and great friends. But somehow, it's not enough. There's this nagging sense that there should be more, that I should be more.

And so, I'm left feeling unfulfilled, always searching for something that I can't quite define. Always wondering if I'm enough, if I'm doing enough, if I'm being enough.

But maybe that's the point. Maybe we're not meant to feel completely fulfilled all the time. Maybe it's that sense of longing, of wanting something more, that drives us forward, that makes us strive to be better.

Maybe it's okay to feel like we're not enough, as long as we keep striving to be better, to do better, to be more fully who we are. Maybe that's what makes us human - the constant struggle to be more, to do more, to live more fully.

So, to anyone out there who feels like they're not enough, who feels unfulfilled and lost - know that you're not alone. Know that it's okay to feel this way, and that it's the struggle to be more that makes life worth living.

COMPANION

My heart's need for a companion
Is my mind's way of belittling the sanity
I crave.

WAKE UP (A POEM FOR QUEENS)

My dear,

Why do you let him play you like this?

Why do you let him spit venom masked as sweet words to you?

Why can't you realize your power?

Do you not know who you are?

Why do you let him put you down?

Why are you so hesitant to put your foot down?

Why can't you see he is no good for you?

"Actions speak louder than words"

And yet, all he has are his words

Words riddled with bullets

Do you not know you are a queen?

And the masses fight for your attention daily

Wake up and realize who you are

You deserve love that will fill you up

Till you can't take no more.

LONG ROAD

The road she's walked is a long one
Sand filled shoes
Thirsty bottles and starved pots
Her clothes stained with tears
Scars from missed destinations
The road she's walked is a long one
And still, there's no end in sight

I GOT FLOWERS TODAY

Flowers are said to be a girl's best friend,

But how can they be,

When they wither and die with time?

Roses, once bright red, turn dark and lonely,

Growing old and shriveled,

Their petals falling day by day.

As I watch this cycle repeat with each flower received,

I can't help but see the unfortunate state of our generation's love life.

I CAN SEE THE LIGHT

I know

I know how it must feel

Not moving at the same pace with your peers

Seeing congratulations everywhere else except your doorstep

Seeing your friends buy houses or cars while you're still struggling with the bus

Hearing babies cry everywhere except your home

I know

I know how hard it feels when you're trying without results

I know how cruel the word *"patience"* can be when that's all you've been

I know how hard it must be not being able to achieve all the goals you've set at a given time

I know

-

"The patient dog gets the fattest bone"

Everyone's path is different

And as hard as it may be to hear that and not see results,

Reality makes it the hard truth

Where you're at right now, is where you're meant to be

This foundation is what gets you to the next level

Your experiences here shape your life for when you get to the level you want to be

"Delay is not denial"

You will get to your destination

But before you do, be grateful for where you are now

We're almost out of the tunnel,

I can see the light.

MONOLOGUE: CAN I BE HONEST I

Some days are harder than others. One moment you're feeling okay and having fun, and the next moment you're questioning everything about your life. It can be tough when people put you on a pedestal because of what they see on social media. You feel like you have to maintain that image, or else you'll be seen as a fraud.

Assumptions can be so destructive. I stopped making assumptions about other people's lives when I realized that my own life was nothing like what others assumed it was. People can put on a mask outside and be the life of the party, but inside, they may be dying.

It's scary and shocking when people say they want to be like me because they think I'm living the dream life.

I hate being put on a pedestal because the same people who put you up there can be the same ones who tear you down once they realize that your life isn't as perfect as they thought it was. Assumptions are a slow killer. Keeping up appearances to impress people who know nothing about your life is not worth it. Everyone has their own struggles and demons to fight, so let's stop holding each other to such high standards and making assumptions about one another.

LOVE & WAR

Unraveling through this twisted phase

My pondering mind and the feelings of my heart

Constantly clashing,

Constantly at war,

The heart wants what it wants, they say

Yet it's as brittle as glass

Once shattered, impossible to fix

It feels as though I'm peeking through a keyhole

Isolated from the outside world by a door

"*Go out and explore*" says the heart

"*Remember what happened the last time you did?*"

My mind retorts

Salient reason to avoid opening that door

—

Loving him is not an option, at least not now

My brittle heart needs respite to recuperate.

Maybe then, the door will be ajar.

DAYDREAMING

What if she dared to confess

To want him all to herself?

What if eternity spent with him,

Didn't seem like a distant dream?

What if their paths intertwined

For a purpose still unknown?

What if they both built walls

To guard against how much they've grown?

What if their flaws and quirks

Made them perfectly imperfect?

What if it's all just in her mind

And he doesn't fit her perfect picture?

REPEAT FEELINGS

You're back here again

This ongoing cycle

Getting played,

Realizing your self-worth,

Being sweet talked into giving multiple chances

Getting played again

It seems you enjoy it

Getting a piece of your heart broken

With each cycle

It seems as if the sound of his sugared lies

Have more melody than the sound of peace your sanity brings

And as you read this

It will feel as if you're ready to break free

Break free from his hold

But just when you think you're in the clear

Your phone will vibrate

"*I miss you*"

And there you'll be

Giving him another chance

Repeating the cycle

ECHOS OF REGRET

Regrets are heavy burdens we carry

Filled with thoughts of what we could have done,

Paths we could have taken or avoided

Chances missed and battles lost

They are little pockets of living in the *"what could have been"*

They haunt us with their endless whispers

Of *"what ifs"*, *"should haves"* and *"could nevers"*,

Reminding us of our past mistakes

And filling us with long lasting doubts

Steps we could or could have never taken

"What if I never did? What if I did?"

-

We can't change the past

Nor do we know the future

We can only hope our present doesn't land us in the repeated cycle of *"what could have been"*

LOST AND FOUND

Of all the things I've lost

I miss my mind the most

It used to be a library of memories and thoughts

But now it's a jumbled mess, a chaotic storm

I struggle to find my way through the fog

And grasp the parts of my scattered mind

I miss the clarity, the ease of thought

When words flowed like a stream

Now they're stuck, tangled in the weeds

I miss the days when my mind was free

-

But perhaps this chaos is not a curse

Maybe it's a new kind of gift

A chance to break old patterns and beliefs

To explore new paths and ways of being

Maybe it's an invitation to be more present

To slow down and savor each moment

And learn to let go of what no longer serves me

To create space for new growth and learning

So even though I miss my old mind

I embrace this new opportunity for change

THE BEST REVENGE

They hurt you.

You felt it deep,

A wound, a scar, a permanent mark.

But here's the thing:

Revenge isn't in the imitation of their actions.

It's not in holding onto that hurt.

The best revenge?

Heal.

Move on.

Don't become them.

That's it.

Simple.

Powerful.

But true.

MONOLOGUE: LET IT OUT

You know, it's completely okay to cry. Tears aren't a sign of weakness; they're a sign that you're human, that you feel deeply. They're a language, a form of expression that says what words sometimes can't.

And in those moments when the world feels too heavy, it's okay to sit still. To be still is not to be stagnant; it's to gather yourself, like the ocean pulling back before the tide rushes in. It's a moment to breathe, to reflect, and to prepare for the next wave of life that's coming your way.

But listen, while you're in that space of quiet, don't lose sight of what's ahead. Remember how far you've traveled, the mountains you've climbed, the rivers you've crossed. You are a living testament to resilience, a walking medley of battles won and lessons learned.

The world can be a harsh critic sometimes, quick to highlight your flaws and eager to bury you in doubt. But you, you are your own masterpiece in progress. Each challenge sculpts you into a more intricate form. You are both the artist and the art, constantly evolving.

So, when life tries to break you, and it will, fight to come out not just intact but transformed. Like a phoenix, use the flames that try to consume you as the fuel to rise again, stronger, brighter, and more brilliant than before.

Cry, sit still, but then rise. Rise because you are a warrior, and warriors are not defined by the battles they lose but by the wars they continue to fight.

MIDNIGHT MUSINGS

SELFISH LOVE

The clock hits 3:02 a.m.

And only the thought of you occupies my mind

My selfish desire to have you all to myself brings me nothing but misery

How could I want something that isn't mine?

How could I want something that could never be mine?

Racing heart, sweaty hands

Butterflies every time your lips fell on mine

Ringing laughter, brilliant smiles

I always look forward to our next encounter

A part of me wants to fight this feeling,

A part of me can't help but fall deeper,

And I'm ashamed to say I want to bask in the glory of this dalliance

I know this is all temporary,

One day, this will all end,

And I'll be shattered

Because you were never mine

But at least I'll have peace knowing I had you in this lifetime

BEAUTIFUL MAN

He was a charmer

Eyes as bright as the sun

Teeth white as an angel clad in light

Lips soft as silk

Every time he looked at me,

His eyes pierced through my soul

As though forcing our souls to become one

His warm kisses sending vibrations through

my body until my legs quivered

His gentle touch, exploring my body like a map

His body in sync with mine

And mine with his

—

We danced body as one

Touch to touch

All through the night

Sheets drenched in the dampness of our encounter

—

I hope we cross paths again

My beautiful man.

FANTASY LOVE

Is this love or is this just fantasy

Floating through the high your presence brings, and I wonder

Is this real?

There's you and there's him

There's him and there's you but I find it hard to recognize

Which is love and which is fantasy?

My mind starts to tease me with glimpses of the passion in your eyes when you look at me,

the warmth of your breath as you kiss down my neck,

the calm I feel as your arms wrap around me,

But then I stop to wonder

Is this love or just fantasy?

HEY, STRANGER

2:20 a.m.

Liquor manipulated thoughts

Torn between dialing your number

Or just sending a text

They say alcohol makes you do dumb things

And of course, the liquor makes excuses for you

Knowing you've done me wrong

Making me think I want you when I don't.

-

Or do I?

-

Glass after glass, just to get you off my mind

But here I am, with you still on my mind

And so, I pick up the phone

"Hey stranger"

IF I HAD A MAN

Tonight, you'll be the artist

And I'll be your muse

Your body against mine

Slow dancing to sweet melodies

Your lips against my neck

Caressing it like a violin

We dance all the way to the boudoir

Bodies sinking into the sheets

Legs interlocked as if in an everlasting tango

Hands exploring all my curves

Breaths deepen

Passion fills the air and time slows down

As if to give way for us

-

Wine filled glass

Discarded bottles of Pinot Grigio

My mind played tricks on me with each sip

Only if I had a man

This wouldn't be a figment of my imagination

SINS OF THE NIGHT

She danced all night in her birthday suit

She tried to drink all her problems away

She accepted open invites from Casanovas

She hoped to drown all misery in the sinkhole the liquor had created,

Even if for a moment

Yet, there was life,

Watching her, not judging her wild antics

Because once morning comes

And she's puked all her sins,

Everything comes back, and the cycle repeats

MONOLOGUE CAN I BE HONEST II

It's hard for me to give love, you know. It's not because I don't want to or because I don't care. It's because of my past.

I've been hurt before. I've been betrayed, lied to, and left behind. I've been told I'm not good enough, that I'm too much, that I'm not worth it. And it's left me with this fear, this fear of giving my love away and being hurt again.

I know it's not fair. I know that not everyone's the same, and that not everyone will hurt me. But that fear, that fear of being hurt, it's hard to shake off.

It's hard for me to open up, to let someone in. It's hard for me to be vulnerable, to show my true self. It's hard for me to trust, to believe that someone won't hurt me.

But I'm trying, you know. I'm trying to let go of my past, to not let it define me. I'm trying to be brave, to take a chance on love. I'm trying to be open, to show my true self. And I'm trying to trust, to believe that someone won't hurt me.

It's not easy, but I'm trying. And I hope that someday, I'll be able to give love freely, without fear or hesitation. Because deep down, I know that love is worth it, and that I'm worth it too.

TIME WILL NOT WAIT FOR YOU

Love while you can, my friend
Hold those dear to you close
Time has no expiry date
And it waits for no one
Cherish every moment
For tomorrow's not guaranteed
And time is fleeting and swift
So, love while you can, my friend
Hug while you can
For time may be unforgiving
But love is the spark that ignites

MY LOVER

Dance with me, my lover

Let's move till our bodies sync to the beat

Till all your focus and gaze sits with me

And your sturdy hands grip my back

Dance with me, my lover

Your eyes aligned with mine

My fingers interlocked around your neck

Your warm breath circling my atmosphere

Your hands slowly exploring my body

And your lips surveying my face

Dance with me, my lover

Don't let go, till I say the word

WINGS OF ENVY

I envy the birds sometimes
Their ability to live free
Their ability to flap their wings and soar
To live free from judgment
To find food wherever and whenever
To live without constraints and rules,
Without worry and in solitude,
I envy the birds sometimes
But I would never wish to be them

EMBRACING SILENCE

In the quiet of the night

I listen to the silence

It's a peaceful quiet

That speaks volumes to my soul

It's the absence of noise

That makes me truly hear –

The whispers of the wind,

The rustle of the leaves,

The sound of my own breath,

Inhaling,

Exhaling,

I feel my heartbeat,

A steady reminder of life

Silence is not empty

It's full of untold stories,

Of memories and dreams,

That only reveal themselves

In the calm of the night

So, I welcome the silence

And let it cover me

A peaceful break from the world's noise

TO BE

In the stillness of her soul,

she finds a sense of peace,

content to simply be.

BOUND BY DESIRE

Come with me, my love

Let's explore these sheets together

Let's drown in the depths of each other

Come witness this river overflow

I want you to bathe in it,

Bask in it,

Let's navigate our body bends together

Solving every puzzle with our hands

Let's swear an oath with our tongues

Promising to never free ourselves from the bosom of each other

Till we find a release button

-

Come with me, my love

Let our souls be intertwined with each other and our burning desire fuel this union

ILLUSIONS OF LUST

In the hidden area of the park,
There he sat, a figure against the sun's path.
Tall, as if he could touch the sky,
Dark, like the mysteries of the night,
Handsome, in a way that made time stand still,
And a smile revealing perfect dentition, white as snow

The world slowed down, and it was just him and the bench,
Every detail of him engraved in my mind
The way his fingers drummed to a silent tune,
The gentle whisper of leaves blowing in the background

In the theatre of my mind, images began to play,
A wedding, our hands intertwined,
Tropical destinations, sunsets,
The promise of a happily ever after.

But as these images grew vivid and intense,
Reality shifted, pulling me back to the present.
I looked up, ready for his gaze to fall on mine
Only to find the bench empty, void of romance.

An illusion in broad daylight.

TIMELESS DEVOTION

I seek a love, gentle yet unwavering,

A love that listens, that understands without words

I yearn for arms that hold me with tenderness,

Eyes that see beyond the mask, breaking down every facade,

A heart in harmony with mine,

Navigating every twist, every hidden path.

Not just a brief encounter, but a consistent warmth,

A love that sees beyond flaws,

That remains steadfast, in every shadow, every ray,

Whispers that comfort, silences that connect,

A bond unbreakable by time or distance,

A love seeking more than just the surface,

A love that fills every empty space,

A love that becomes the rhythm and the song

A love that soothes, a love that heals,

Turning every challenge into a shared grace.

A love that gives meaning to every detail,

Promising to be there, till the very end.

RISING FROM THE ASHES

SCARS AND STARDUST

These scars upon my heart,

planted by the touch of love and loss,

linger long after the wounds have healed.

I trace them with my fingertips,

memorizing the stories they tell,

each one a reminder of the pain I've felt.

They remind me of the risks I've taken,

the battles I've fought,

the love that was worth the cost.

They are my badges of honor,

proof that I've loved and lost,

but also, that I have survived.

As I look upon these scars,

I am reminded that my heart is resilient,

That it can endure and heal.

So, I wear them with pride,

these scars,

for they have made me who I am.

THEY HEARD YOU

Unleash your caged thoughts

Release your mind from torture

They see you now,

No more running,

No more hiding,

They're listening now.

Though it seemed like hope was lost,

Though you felt like a ticking time bomb

Waiting to explode at any moment,

Though the darkness was overwhelming,

You made it here, your call for help was answered

LET GO

Remove your finger from the trigger
The war is over, the battle done
Your shattered pieces
Will be made whole once more
The hurt and scars, the torments
Shall be healed to the core

NEW BEGINNINGS

Standing on the empty sandy shore,

Clothed in relief and contentment,

The wind caressed her neck with every turn,

And the whispers of the birds grew louder.

The skies were blue again,

And the sun shone brighter than ever before,

Her eyes regained their lost glow,

What was this feeling?

Maybe this was the sign she sought,

That she had become whole again,

That the pain and sorrow had been left behind,

And she was finally free to unwind.

ALL THE THINGS YOU ARE

You embody beauty,

Grace, and charisma.

A single glance turns heads in a room,

As birds chirp with joy at your sight.

You possess a power others can only dream of.

You're a hill of blooming flowers on a winter's

night,

One of a kind, a rare sight to behold.

THE ACT OF FREEDOM

Run away, love

Leave your mark on the sands of time, love

Uncover your hidden gifts, love

Open your heart with honesty and trust, love

Embrace the magic you radiate, love

Speak your truth and live it, love

For the world is fleeting,

The tide is retreating,

The fire is fading,

Time is not on your side.

So run away, love,

Be free.

I AM

I am love,

Divine and beautiful,

Powerful and deserving,

Worthy of everything there is to love.

I am a force to be reckoned with,

Perfectly imperfect in all my glory,

All the things money can't buy.

I am strong,

I am capable,

I am worthy of love,

I am intelligent,

I am confident,

I am in control of my life,

I am worthy of happiness,

I am enough.

CONSTANT REMINDER

I seek a constant reminder

That my past does not define me.

It is not a mirror of my identity,

For I've evolved into a new being.

I'm a new entity, born anew,

Awakened from my slumber.

No longer do sharp words cut deep,

Or manipulation move me under.

I am reborn, unbound and free,

No longer held captive by my past.

For I've stepped into a new destiny,

And found a life worth living.

May this reminder be a source of strength,

To carry me through each new day.

And may it also be a reminder,

That I am not my past in any way.

RADIANT RESILIENCE

Do you not know that you are a light that shines so bright,

Just like the blazing sun, a force of nature,

A heart as pure as the snow,

With beauty that's clear for the world to see.

Your strength is like a mighty wave,

That crashes through the doubts.

You are resilient through and through

With the power to achieve all you believe in

Your heart is so full of love,

And your soul is the purest form of authenticity.

-

And when the world feels like a test,

When it feels as if everything is crashing down,

Remember that you are not your failure

So, you will rise above it

And when you doubt your strength and grace,

Remember that you are beautiful,

And that your light will always shine,

For all the world to see

MONOLOGUE: ALMOST THERE

I never thought I'd get here, you know. To this point where I almost feel free. It's been a long road, full of ups and downs, twists and turns. But somehow, I made it.

I remember when I used to feel so trapped, so stuck. Like I was living someone else's life, and I couldn't break free. I was living in fear, in shame, in guilt. I was holding onto things that weren't serving me, that were weighing me down.

But then something shifted. Something changed. Maybe it was a person, or a moment, or a realization. Maybe it was a combination of things. But whatever it was, it helped me to see things in a new light.

I started to let go of the things that were holding me back. I started to release the shame, the guilt, the fear. I started to forgive myself for the mistakes I'd made, and to see myself in a new way. I started to embrace my true self, my authentic self, and to live my life on my own terms.

It wasn't easy, you know. It took a lot of work, a lot of tears, a lot of hard conversations with myself. But it was worth it. Because now, I almost feel free.

I still have moments where I feel trapped, where I feel stuck. I still have fears and doubts and insecurities. But they don't define me anymore. They don't control me anymore. And that's what makes me feel free.

I'm not there yet, you know. I'm not fully free. But I'm closer than I've ever been. And that gives me hope, that gives me strength, that gives me the courage to keep going.

So, here's to the journey, to the ups and downs, to the twists and turns. Here's to the moments where we almost feel free. Because those moments, those are the moments that make it all worth it.

STANDING IN THE MIRROR

She looks in the mirror

and sees a reflection

of a woman at peace.

Gone are the doubts,

the fears, the insecurities,

They are now replaced with a quiet confidence.

She is comfortable in her own skin,

knowing that she is perfect

just as she is.

The noise of the world fades away,

and in the stillness, she hears

the gentle voice of her own soul.

It whispers words of love and acceptance,

reminding her that she is whole,

that she is complete.

And in this moment,

she is at peace with herself,

finding joy in the simple act of being.

DEFINE

She refuses to be defined
by the opinions of others.

She knows that the only voice that truly matters
is the one inside her own head.

She listens to that voice,
cultivating her own sense of worth and value,
finding strength in her own beliefs.
No longer moved by the judgments of others,
she stands tall and proud,
confident in the knowledge that she is enough,
exactly as she is.

She knows that true happiness and fulfillment
come not from pleasing others,
but from being true to herself,
from honoring her own dreams and desires.

And so she walks through the world,
a beacon of self-assurance and strength,

refusing to be defined by anyone else's standards,

finding joy and freedom in the knowledge

that she is the only one who can define who she truly is.

OCEAN BREEZE

The ocean stretches out before her,

endless and wide,

the waves crashing against the shore.

She stands there,

feeling the breeze in her face,

the air filling her lungs,

her worries and fears carried away by the wind.

For a moment,

all is still and quiet,

the only sound, the rush of the water.

She breathes in the peace of the moment,

letting it fill her up,

letting it wash away the stresses of the day,

the doubts and fears that so often consume her.

For a moment,

she is free,

free from the pressures of the world.

In this moment,

standing on the ocean shore,

she is at peace,

her heart and soul quiet and still,

her spirit renewed and refreshed.

And she knows,

as the waves continue to crash against the shore,

that this moment will stay with her,

a reminder of the peace and beauty that exists in the world,

a reminder of the power of the natural world to heal and renew,

a reminder of the strength that resides within her.

SHEDDING

She's shed the weight of her past,
letting go of the burdens
that held her down for so long.

She's stepped into the light of her present,
embracing the freedom
that comes with being true to herself.

No longer held captive by the expectations of others,
she moves through the world with a new sense of purpose,
a new sense of possibility.

She is free to love who she wants,
to live how she wants,
to be who she is.

And in this freedom,
she finds a sense of peace,
a sense of joy,
that fills her up from the inside out.

No longer a prisoner of her own fears,

She walks with her head held high.

So, here's to her journey,

to the struggles and the triumphs,

to the moments that have brought her here.

May she continue to find the courage to be free,

to embrace her true self,

and to live life on her own terms.

LET'S TALK ...

She used to be a people pleaser, always putting the wants and needs of others before her own. It had become a way of life for her, always thinking that sacrificing her own happiness was the right thing to do. She would bend over backwards for people, trying to make them happy, but it never seemed to be enough.

One day, she woke up and realized that she was tired of it all. She was tired of constantly putting others first and not taking care of herself. It wasn't that she didn't care about the people in her life, it was just that she realized she needed to prioritize her own happiness and well-being.

She felt a sense of guilt at first, thinking that being selfish was a bad thing. But then she realized that it wasn't about being selfish, it was about taking care of herself. She needed to set boundaries and learn how to say no, even if it meant disappointing people.

It was a difficult transition, but she started to notice a change in herself. She felt more confident and less anxious. She was able to focus on her own goals and aspirations and started to feel a sense of fulfillment.

Of course, there were times when she still felt guilty for saying no or putting herself first, but she reminded herself that it was necessary for her own well-being. She learned that taking care of herself first allowed her to take better care of the people she loved.

Now, she still cares about the people in her life, but she knows that her own happiness and well-being is just as important. She's no longer a people pleaser, and that's okay. She's learning to put herself first, and that's a beautiful thing.

POTRAITS OF PEACE

Maybe it's a quiet day all to yourself,

Losing track of time in a good book,

Taking time for a spa, just because,

Shopping alone, at your own pace,

Or traveling by yourself, no plans in place.

Sometimes, peace is blocking out the world,

Finding joy in a hobby, day after day,

Booking a hotel room, just to breathe.

Maybe it's watching a movie at home,

A solo dinner, where your thoughts are undisturbed,

Learning to love yourself, again and again.

Peace can look different for everyone.

What does peace look like for you?

STRENGTH THROUGH THE STORM

Look at you,

able to laugh and breathe once more,

to love with a heart that's been torn,

Look at you weathering the storm.

Look how you dodge the stones life throws,

rising after countless blows,

opening up and loving yourself,

being gentle with yourself once again.

-

Yes, the storm will come,

harsh realities will test your resolve,

you'll fall and struggle to get up,

but as long as you're alive,

Don't stop fighting,

Don't stop trying,

Don't stop living,

Don't stop loving.

FREE AT LAST

…And just like the
caterpillar,
Blossoming into the butterfly,
She was full of life
No more hidden wings
No more stalled flights
She was free at last

LOVE LETTERS

DEAR YOUNGER ME,

If I could fold this note into a paper airplane and send it flying back through the years, I would. I'd aim it straight for your open window, where you sit dreaming big dreams and nursing small wounds.

Firstly, know this—you were never at fault for leading with your heart. Your heart, so full and so brave, is not a liability; it's your superpower. It's the compass that guides you, even when it leads you through storms and thorny paths. Don't regret the times it made you vulnerable; celebrate the courage it gave you to love, to feel, and to grow.

You're brave, braver than you'll ever know at that age. The things you've experienced would weigh down souls twice your age, but you? You carry them like feathers on the wings of your ambition. You turn them into wind beneath you, lifting you higher, pushing you to go further.

And for the times you think you've failed, for the moments you feel like you've fallen short, I forgive you. I forgive you for ever thinking you needed validation from anyone else. I forgive you for ever doubting that you're more than enough just as you are. When people ask what you bring to the table, remember this: you are the whole damn table.

You deserve the freedom to move forward without the chains of past regrets holding you back. So, keep leading with that big, beautiful heart of yours. Keep being brave, keep feeling deeply, and keep turning your challenges into steppingstones. One day, you'll look back and realize that every choice, every tear, every laugh, and every struggle was a brushstroke in the masterpiece that is you.

With all the love and wisdom I've gained,

Your Older Self

"HOW WOULD YOU LIKE TO BE LOVED?"

In ways unbeknownst to me,

With all my perfect imperfections,

Intentionally, wholly,

Without limits or restrictions,

Without conditions,

Freely, loudly,

To the ends of the earth and back,

Without a doubt,

Without coercion or hesitation,

Beyond my knowing,

Despite my flaws,

Consistently, unconditionally,

Unapologetically.

Because of who I am

and who I have come to be.

TOO MUCH

I crave the rhythm of your heart

The pulse of life that beats within

I long to touch your very soul

And feel the essence of your being

Let me bear witness to your scars

For they are part of who you are

Let me bask in your presence

Absorbing the light that you impart

I want to sing your praises high

To the heavens and beyond the sky

Is that too much to ask, my dear?

SWEET LOVE

When the sun is down

And the night is out to play

You're the only thing that creeps into my mind

When the world is silent

And the skies are gray

You're the only light that leads my way

You filter out my flaws

And hide my imperfections

You're all I need and all I ever needed is you

You are the only wonder of my world,

Sweet love.

A PRAYER FOR YOU

May your days be filled with roses,

Those that never wither,

And blue skies,

Clear as crystal waters,

May your days never get as dry as the desert sand,

Or as hot as the earth's core,

May the wind hear your wishes,

And blow them up to the heavens,

May the walls keep your secrets,

And protect them within

And may you never see another dark cloud

But only rainbows and clear skies

LETTER TO MY UNBORN (a poem for V)

Raindrops tapping on the windowpane

The sound of distant babies crying

Hands hovering over her tummy

Thinking of what might have been

Of what they could have been

Of the love that could have been their foundation

Their souls intertwined

A love so strong, life growing inside

She would have given everything to protect them

To trade her life for theirs

But now, a few weeks from that fated day

She's left with the memory of what could have been

Of eyes that never met, of bodies that never connected

A newly gained angel

And though her heart aches, she releases the pain

Until the day they meet again.

A MOTHER'S LOVE (a poem for my mum)

The love of a mother is like no other,

fierce and uncompromising,

Steadfast and true.

It is a love that knows no bounds,

that transcends time and space,

that stretches far beyond the limits of this world.

It is a love that is selfless,

that puts the needs of others before its own,

that sacrifices and endures,

even in the face of great pain and hardship.

It is a love that is powerful,

that has the ability to heal and to nurture,

to comfort and to guide,

to shape and to mold.

It is a love that is eternal,

a bond that cannot be broken,

a connection that remains strong and unwavering,

even in the face of adversity and loss.

The love of a mother

a thing of beauty and power,

a testament to the strength and resilience of the human heart.

WHAT WOULD IT FEEL LIKE TO FIND GENUINE LOVE?

It'll be in the way our glances linger longer than they should, so long that I lose myself in the depth of his eyes. A gaze that seems to see straight into my soul, making me wonder what thoughts dance behind those eyes.

It's in the way he'll hold me, with strong, protective, yet inviting arms. It's in the constant craving of being enveloped in his embrace, where the outside world disappears and it's just us. A sense of safety there that I've always longed for.

It'll be the gentle forehead kisses that steal my breath away. Each one a promise, a whisper of affection that resonates through me. In these simple acts, I want to feel most undone, swept away by the tender assurance of his feelings.

I want thoughts of him to constantly occupy my mind, filling the spaces between moments. I crave for that gentle tug at my heart that I can't ignore.

And then there'll be his voice, constantly soothing the chaos in my mind. I picture it being soft and calming, carrying a melody that wraps around me, a comfort I didn't know I needed. It'll be in the way he speaks, the way his laughter changes the atmosphere, and the quiet words shared in the silence, where I find a peace I've longed for.

And in the end, I just want to find a love where I can feel truly at home, lost in the wonder of us.

LETTER TO MY READERS, PART I

Dear Friends,

I understand that life has been challenging for you lately. It seems as though you have been dealt a difficult hand. I know that at times it may feel like everything is overwhelming and that you cannot catch a break.

But please remember, it will get better. There is always a light at the end of the tunnel, and you are closer to it than you think. The struggles you are facing now are temporary, and they will eventually pass.

Do not let your current situation consume you. Instead, let it guide you towards growth and maturity. Although the waters may be turbulent now, know that the shore is within reach. You will make it through this, and you will come out even stronger on the other side.

Your Friend,

Ebose x

LETTER TO MY READERS, PART II

Dear Friends,

I understand how you feel. It's hard when it seems like life keeps knocking you down no matter what you do. It's frustrating when you make compromises, and it still doesn't work out.

But remember, you don't have to lower your standards to meet anyone halfway. You deserve someone who meets your standards and treats you the way you deserve to be treated.

The universe isn't punishing you, and you're not paying for the sins of your ancestors. Life is just difficult sometimes, but it's also full of beauty and joy. Keep pushing forward and focusing on the good things in life. Without struggles, we would never get the experience needed for us to reach our success.

I wish I could tell you exactly what to do to stop feeling this way, but unfortunately, that's something only you can figure out. Just know that you're not alone in feeling this way, and there is always hope for a brighter tomorrow.

Your friend,

Ebose x

REMEMBER

- ★ Take a deep breath and center yourself.
- ★ Acknowledge your feelings without judgment.
- ★ Remember that you've overcome tough times before.
- ★ Focus on the present moment and what you can control.
- ★ Reach out to someone you trust for support.
- ★ Practice self-care and give yourself grace.
- ★ Set small goals and celebrate your accomplishments.
- ★ Remember that your worth is not based on your productivity.
- ★ Keep a gratitude journal and focus on the good in your life.
- ★ Believe in yourself and trust that things will get better.
- ★ You are not defined by your mistakes or failures.
- ★ You are a work in progress, and that is okay.
- ★ God created you for a greater purpose.

Dear Friends,

As I come to the end of this journey, I can't help but feel grateful for having this opportunity to share my words with you. This poetry book is not just a collection of poems, but it is a reflection of my soul, a journey of self-discovery and healing.

I hope that as you read through the pages, you have found comfort in knowing that you are not alone in your struggles, your pain, or your journey towards healing. Each poem I've shared with you has a piece of my heart and my experiences, and I hope that they have resonated with you in some way.

Through the heartbreak, the struggles, and the pain, I hope that you have found hope, strength, and courage. I hope that my words have served as a reminder that you are capable of healing, of finding peace, and of rising above the challenges that come your way.

I want to thank you for taking the time to read my words, for opening your hearts to my stories, and for allowing me to be a part of your journey. It is my sincerest hope that this book has inspired you to embrace your journey, to honor your experiences, and to never give up on yourself.

Remember, healing is not a linear path, and it may not be an easy journey, but it is possible. Keep fighting, keep moving forward, and know that you are not alone.

Until we meet again,

With love and gratitude,

Ebose x